How Teachers Learn Best

An Ongoing Professional Development Model

Edward P. Fiszer

D1602255

ScarecrowEducation
Lanham, Maryland • Toronto • Oxford
2004

Published in the United States of America
by ScarecrowEducation
An imprint of The Rowman & Littlefield Publishing Group, Inc.
4501 Forbes Boulevard, Suite 200, Lanham, Maryland 20706
www.scarecroweducation.com

PO Box 317
Oxford
OX2 9RU, UK

British Library Cataloguing in Publication Information Available

Library of Congress Cataloging-in-Publication Data

Fiszer, Edward P. (Edward Peter), 1970–
   How teachers learn best : an ongoing professional development model /
Edward P. Fiszer.
      p. cm.
   Includes bibliographical references (p.   ) and index.
   ISBN 1-57886-070-9 (pbk. : alk. paper)
   1. Teachers—In-service training. 2. Career development. 3. Experiential
learning. I. Title.
LB1731 .F49 2003
370'.71'5—dc21
                                                                  2003011522

∞™ The paper used in this publication meets the minimum requirements of
American National Standard for Information Sciences—Permanence of
Paper for Printed Library Materials, ANSI/NISO Z39.48-1992.
Manufactured in the United States of America.

To have his path made clear for him is the aspiration of every human being in our beclouded and tempestuous existence.

—Joseph Conrad

To live is the rarest thing in the world. Most people exist, that is all.

—Oscar Wilde

All things are ready, if our minds be so.

—*Henry V*, William Shakespeare

Contents

Contents

Preface to Chapters 5, 6, and 7: Lessons from Teachers

Teacher focus groups were asked to discuss their views on teacher learning. Twenty-seven teachers were interviewed from three elementary schools in Los Angeles County. Chapters 5, 6, and 7 focus on teacher input on a process that they rarely are given the forum to discuss openly. The comments of these teachers in connection with the current professional development research inspired the fourteen recommendations found in chapter 9.

Table P.1 gives an overview of the key issues and concepts discussed during the focus group as well as the percentage of teachers in agreement with the issues. Because each individual was not obligated to respond to the discussion questions, the number in the left-hand column represents those who spoke in agreement with the statement as a percentage/fraction of the total who responded.

Table P.1.   A Sampling of Key Ideas and Issues Discussed during Focus Groups

Percentage in Agreement	
82%	Peer observation is a beneficial professional development strategy.
70%	Experienced teachers are not typically offered opportunities to observe other teachers.
77%	Opportunities for reflection and dialogue are rare.
59%	The need for dialogue exists to solve problems and vent frustrations.
15%	Discomfort arises for those who wish to bring up negatives during dialogue sessions in which administrators are present.
56%	Reflection and dialogue cannot solely happen in the staff lounge but need to be incorporated into the regular school schedule.
59%	Reflection and dialogue opportunities build camaraderie.
52%	Constructive feedback from an experienced practitioner is an asset to professional development.

Introduction: Why Is Ongoing Professional Development Necessary? or Are You an Educational Lewis and Clark?

If working alone, you may be solely a "Lewis" or just a "Clark" by the time this discussion is concluded. However, the idea is there: Lewis and Clark proceeding into uncharted territory—valiant, brave, and tenacious—despite the danger and slim odds of success.

Why would a discussion of ongoing professional development warrant such an image? Teachers live, work, and interact with many people yet are alone in professional terms. Those who have taught, especially teachers in elementary education, know that teaching is often synonymous with isolation.

Teachers are rarely watched by anyone but their students and as a result are often put off when a visitor is in the room. Visits by administrators for more than a few minutes are typically scheduled in advance. The opportunity to watch or be observed by other practitioners is rare. Receiving feedback and interacting with colleagues in a way that sharpens professional skills is unusual.

A professional achieves a certain level of expertise in an area of study and is expected to keep current within the field. Auto mechanics, dentists, and truck drivers must prove themselves to be current in their professions. Is a method of keeping teachers' skills current and alive within their profession commonly in place? Not by a long shot.

The reality about traditional professional development for teachers is that it is often taught using methods not aligned with active learning. Teachers typically sit and listen to an expert who advocates active, hands-on learning for students but puts little of this talk into practice. Furthermore, the topics are not close to relevant. This style of professional development is not only hypocritical and agonizing but outdated and a disservice to professional educators. Teachers deserve better and can have what they need in a relatively inexpensive manner—by being given the time and wherewithal to learn from one another. Ongoing professional development fosters the kind of support teachers do not have within their traditional culture of isolation.

This is why any district administrator, superintendent, site administrator, teacher, parent, school board member, or community activist who remotely agrees with the proposed recommendations in this book is a "Lewis" or a "Clark." Do something about this. Help teachers communicate with one another. This rarely charted territory provides possibilities in the face of obstacles. For example, rather than viewing the creation of release time for teachers as impossible, find a way to have an experienced teacher or administrator read a story to a class while the classroom teacher visits another room. With a small amount of effort, the recommendations in this book can become at least a small-scale reality. The benefits will be tangible among those who participate. The energy level of those who meet together to discuss student work samples, perhaps voluntarily after school, will surprise many. The emergence of ideas among teachers is not uncommon—once they are allowed the time to interact.

The initial reaction to change is resistance. An old proverb states that any solution contains the seeds of future problems. Starting with a massive top-down fiat forcing all teachers to visit one another, however, removes the feel of benefit. I suggest a voluntary beginning to any of the recommendations in this book. Unfortunately, innovative professional development is more similar to a grassroots effort than a large-scale one in most parts of the United States. What begins on a small scale can take root in a way that those involved can see the resulting concerns that will come up and trim the tree to stimulate more growth as time passes.

Ongoing professional development is necessary. Teachers need to refresh one another with ideas and suggestions that cannot be provided through an agenda item at a staff meeting. Children deserve a professional who can go to colleagues to discuss problems encountered in the classroom.

NOTES ON THE STUDY

The study yielding the data upon which the recommendations are based was conducted as part of the Educational Leadership Program at UCLA.

Teachers from three public elementary schools in Los Angeles County were interviewed in a focus-group format. Nine tenured teachers from each school participated. All participants were candid during the interviews.

This study endeavored to reveal whether teachers believe professional development components such as reflective dialogue and peer observation can positively impact their teaching. The literature recommends these components, as well as an environment open to professional discussion, peer coaching and observation, and other methods of analyzing and stretching the craft of each teacher. The literature emphasizes a laboratory environment where teachers recognize their environment as learning enriched rather than learning impoverished. If professional development is part of the organization and structure of the school, then a culture of ongoing professional development can be reached. The teachers in this study provided an excellent starting point for the shift in structure from one-shot, atheoretical, passive professional development sessions to sustained, active, theory-based activities that are part of an ongoing professional development culture.

Because there is a high correlation between literature recommendations and the professional development components of the schools in this study, a qualitative study examining teacher perceptions of professional development will be useful to practitioners. The intent was to find out if teachers perceive the structure of professional development they were receiving as effective, including forms of reflective dialogue, peer observation, and consistent feedback. The study clarifies how key professional development elements may be used as part of professional development training. Site administrators can use teacher perceptions to avoid pitfalls as ongoing professional development programs are developed at their schools.

The intent of this qualitative study was to analyze teacher perceptions of professional development. Professional development is too often not an integral part of the structure of the school. It is frequently a one-time-only experience that does not provide useful feedback to teachers on a regular basis. There is a need to demonstrate support for teachers and to influence their learning.

Chapter One

How Do Teachers Learn Best?

Traditional teacher professional development too often prevents teachers from maximizing their learning. Educational leaders must generate a cultural shift to an ongoing model of professional development if teacher learning is a priority. The implementation of a model incorporating peer observations, dialogue, and feedback enlivens the profession for both new and experienced teachers.

The traditional professional development model primarily fails because newly introduced pedagogies are not consistently incorporated into actual practice. To impact teacher behavior through professional development programs, educational leaders need to acknowledge teacher perceptions regarding professional development. Although the research literature advocates the use of such programs, it has, until now, been unclear if or how teachers perceive these key components as essential to their learning. This book examines teacher perceptions of professional development containing key elements studied in research literature. The resulting data point to the need for an ongoing professional development model that directly connects training and practice. Strategies to support this type of model are advocated by educational leaders in the concluding chapter.

A vibrant connection between training and practice can be maintained through a cultural shift away from top-down, dialogue-free sessions toward an ongoing model of teacher professional development. Typical top-down sessions are remedial, quick fixes for weak areas or single sessions without ongoing feedback to the practitioners. They are often based on a deficiency model, in which sessions focus on a single skill or attribute that teachers appear to lack. Research over the past few decades

1

on instructional improvement indicates that single-session programs are largely ineffective.

There is a need for educational leaders to address the perceptions of teachers in order to effectively meet teacher professional development needs. Teachers are rarely given the opportunity to voice their opinions on professional development in a meaningful way. Typically, a single professional development session ends with a one-page evaluation form where teachers check boxes to indicate their level of satisfaction with the presenter and, if they care to, leave a comment on the session. As clear as some literature recommendations are, it is important to confirm the validity of these ideas with current teachers. Once confirmed, it would be a logical step for educational leaders to utilize the information to plan effective learning experiences for their teachers. Therefore, the following question needed to be addressed: What do teachers consider characteristic of meaningful learning experiences?

> **There is a need for educational leaders to address the perceptions of teachers in order to effectively meet teacher professional development needs.**

Teachers generally cannot connect professional development programs to classroom practice because ongoing programs correlated with practice are atypical. Professional development requires modeling, practice in simulated and actual settings, and structured, open-ended feedback about performance observed during actual practice. Effective professional development should ensure follow-up to the ideas discussed where collaboration, testing of selected ideas, and reflective practice are involved. Unfortunately, the expressed needs of teachers are not evident in typical professional development programs.

During traditional professional development workshops, there is no forum for discussion of the trial and error of the ideas after they are put into practice. Too often, no structured method is in place to help teachers improve practice by encouraging them to interact with or watch other colleagues in action (Little 1999). The learning needs to be ongoing, interactive, and supportive to the teacher. Merely watching a presenter isn't enough.

> **During traditional professional development workshops, there is no forum for discussion of the trial and error of the ideas after they are put into practice.**

Teachers in this study clarified how an ongoing professional development program influenced their learning. Once given an opportunity to describe their learning experiences, teachers revealed additional insights into ongoing professional development. Teachers do not often have the opportunity to observe peers during classroom practice, an event that can influence teachers more so than the average professional development speaker (Meier 1992). Reflective conversations are not routine and are often discounted in favor of top-down faculty meetings where teachers rarely participate in dialogue. Exploring a topic in a concentrated manner over time and receiving consistent feedback regarding practice are not common events in teacher professional development. Those who have been offered these types of support describe a positive impact on their classroom practice.

This work helps fill the gap left by a lack of documentation on how teachers perceive ongoing professional development. Teacher perceptions were based on a professional development environment, one that has shifted from previous status quo training sessions to a new structure for such ongoing professional development.

The teachers who participated in this study were involved in ongoing professional development programs that follow the philosophy that knowledge is constructed through experience (Brooks and Brooks 1993). The word *experience* is derived from the Latin *experiri*, meaning to try or put to the test. Teachers may feel that a half-day workshop can be a meaningful experience based on the usual feedback questionnaire passed out at the end of the session. But those teachers need to test what they heard, namely to "experience" the ideas. After the ideas are put to the test, the real impact on the teacher would likely come when he or she reflects on what has occurred and compares experiences with other practitioners.

A variety of perceptions exist that might be useful to the educational community. Educational leaders need the point of view of teachers, not simply researchers, to plan and implement an effective and meaningful professional development program in an elementary school context.

Teachers might support the literature and agree that the components of dialogue, peer observation, and consistent feedback create a meaningful experience. Teachers might be neutral and indifferent to the entire new structure. Or teachers might perceive this shift negatively because they encountered too much conversation about the program and prefer isolation. In addition to professional development, teachers might identify nonacademic benefits, such as making more friends on the staff or having opportunities to vent and brainstorm for ways beyond program difficulties. If the professional development structure does not have the positive impact the literature indicates, teachers interviewed can say why the experience was not positive, explain what they would change, describe if there is a nonacademic impact, or discuss any other positive or negative experiences. A focus-group format was used to give teachers the opportunity to candidly describe their experiences.

At the conclusion of each chapter, the reader will find reflective questions to help make the ideas come alive. The reader is viewed as an educational leader at a school site. Since any individual can have an impact at the site level regardless of position, all readers are encouraged to review the considerations at the ends of the chapters with their individual school setting in mind.

CONSIDERATIONS ADDRESSED BY SUCCESSFUL PROFESSIONAL DEVELOPMENT PROGRAMS

1. Are teachers involved in the planning of professional development at your site?
2. In what areas would teachers like feedback?
3. Which key staff members will you interact with as you adjust professional development to an ongoing model?
4. Who will give honest criticism to ideas and help brainstorm?

Chapter Two

Traditional Professional Development

Traditional professional development activities often provide insufficient opportunities for teacher learning. Teaching for understanding requires educators to see complex subject matter from the perspectives of diverse students. This understanding cannot come from prepackaged professional development or conveyed by means of traditional top-down teacher training strategies. Too often, professional development training sessions are not based on expressed teacher needs but on a remediation and quick-fix mentality. Teachers consider it a waste of time to listen to "outside experts" talk about teaching skills that infrequently connect to the current problems encountered in the classrooms. To sustain teacher learning that directly affects classroom practice, we must provide a culture that requires and supports ongoing professional development.

> **Too often, professional development training sessions are not based on expressed teacher needs but on a remediation and quick-fix mentality.**

TYPICAL PROBLEMS WITH TRADITIONAL PROFESSIONAL DEVELOPMENT

Professional development programs do not lend themselves to an integrated learning experience for teachers when they lack ongoing training linked to a shared vision of the school, reflective dialogue, peer observation, and feedback. Most teachers who have not received feedback on implementation of

5

the new teaching strategies soon forget them. Too many professional development sessions are planned efforts where educators "sit relatively passively while an expert exposes them to new ideas or trains them in new practices, and the success of the effort is judged by a 'happiness quotient' that measures participants' satisfaction with the experience and their off-the-cuff assessment regarding its usefulness" (Sparks 1997, 1).

The problem of passive training is recognized in the business world as well. Peter Senge, a leading author in the area of organizational learning, defines learning as the enhancement of capacity through experience gained by following a track or discipline. He explains that the best arena for learning is in real-life settings that matter to the learner, not in training sessions or classrooms. Learning in an active rather than passive context enhances capacity for effective action and generates knowledge that lasts (Senge 1999). Since active learning strategies are atypical, those within the school will notice the intent of the professional development. The organization of active learning activities viewed by participants as beneficial is a major step toward creating a culture where ongoing learning is valued.

To avoid meaningless "one time only" professional development problems, there must be a transformation from a single program or activity to an ethos (Renyi 1998). This ethos is ideally a school culture where learning is suffused throughout teachers' working lives. However, teachers are all too often not involved in the planning of professional development activities nor are they engaged in any ongoing professional development program.

Planning in Current Teacher Needs

Professional development includes an eclectic collection of activities and programs that vary widely in source of initiation and responsibility, function, and practices of implementation. These activities are so dispersed that many go unnoticed by school district administrators who often do not attend the professional development sessions. Therefore, a direct connection must be established between expressed teacher needs and development planning. To directly impact student learning, teachers must have their needs met during professional development activities. Teachers must be involved in the planning process.

Any school's professional development activities should reflect teacher needs. Teachers who are initially involved in professional development planning have greater commitment and "buy in" to the program. Teachers incorporated into the process can specifically state areas of concern that, when addressed in a practical manner, can directly affect their students. Since a flow of practical suggestions can continuously help teachers, there should be movement toward *continuous* professional development.

Support is essential to developmental growth. As new learning takes place in a professional development program, ongoing personal support should be available so the learner feels understanding, empathy, and warm personal regard. Logically, the best support would come from peers who are in a position to collaborate as a result of the ongoing professional development model.

Ongoing Support of Practices

The idea of ongoing professional development goes against the manner in which sessions have been organized over the years, including the length of the sessions, the topics, and the types of teachers the sessions intend to reach. Research on instructional improvement indicates that programs consisting of a single session are largely ineffective. Professional development as remediation is an outdated model. Rather than as a presentation for teachers deficient in certain skills or attributes, professional development should be based on the expressed needs of teachers that have become known through the planning structure where teacher voices are heard and incorporated into the details of the plan.

> **Research on instructional improvement indicates that programs consisting of a single session are largely ineffective.**

Not only must teachers be involved in determining the theories or strategies presented but professional development activities must also model skills, provide practice opportunities in simulated and actual settings, and allow structured and open-ended feedback about performance. Professional development is most influential when ongoing support of the sessions involves collaboration, testing of selected ideas, reflective practice, and peer observation.

Professional development efforts must include ongoing support aspects such as dialogue and peer observation. Realistic demonstrations with hard-to-teach students should be included to provide a concrete example of how the innovation is to be carried out while creating the basis for further discussion. Without ongoing training, the concepts presented cannot become a permanent part of the school culture.

> **Realistic demonstrations with hard-to-teach students should be included to provide a concrete example of how the innovation is to be carried out while creating the basis for further discussion.**

Minimal time allotted for professional development can be at least partially to blame for the lack of ongoing support activities. Teachers traditionally feel their work time is only time spent in front of the class and that any other work-related activities are "extra." A report by the Delaware State Education Association states ongoing support activities through reflection, dialogue, peer observation, and other strategies are the "single most important and necessary resource for effective school improvement" (DSEA 1994, 2).

Ongoing training and support has not only recently come into the discussion in relation to teacher professional development. The Rand Change Agent Study, conducted from 1973 to 1978, examined professional development in the context of broader change efforts. The study found implementation strategies that fostered teacher learning had two complementary components: staff training activities and training support activities. Each component functions distinctly: skill-specific training in isolation works only in the short run while staff support activities were necessary to sustain the gains of how-to-do-it training (McLaughlin 1991).

If teachers and administrators are not supportive of one another from the outset, then the effort will produce frustration rather than positive results. When professional development is designed properly, virtually all teachers can learn powerful and complex teaching strategies. Without the crucial follow-up support system in place, however, learning connected to practice will not take place.

CONSIDERATIONS ADDRESSED BY SUCCESSFUL PROFESSIONAL DEVELOPMENT PROGRAMS

1. Is teacher learning a part of the school culture or is professional development rarely discussed?
2. Are teachers currently given structured time to collaborate? What follow-up support has been provided for new methods or ideas?
3. Do you know of any examples of single-session professional development programs that your teachers attended without follow-up support? If the topic or strategy discussed was put into practice, did everyone follow through? What helped make that transition from theory to practice happen?

Chapter Three

A Collaborative Culture

Implementation of ongoing professional development requires a school culture that works collaboratively, is adaptable to change, and has a shared understanding of purpose. The shift from isolation to public collaboration intensifies a sense that all instructional staff are in the same boat and trying to accomplish the same goals. Public acknowledgement among staff of the strengths, weaknesses, and obstacles of the school clarifies the direction of the needed professional development. The anxiety common to implementation of new innovations is lessened through the support that peers provide one another. The learning becomes deeply rooted since individuals are not left adrift in isolation but focused through collaboration.

> **The shift from isolation to public collaboration intensifies a sense that all instructional staff are in the same boat and trying to accomplish the same goals. Public acknowledgement among staff of the strengths, weaknesses, and obstacles of the school clarifies the direction of the needed professional development.**

COLLABORATION

To implement ongoing professional development, the school needs to function collaboratively. The school's social climate, attitudes, and patterns of behavior influence the learning of both teachers and students. Research is filled with information on the importance of developing a collaborative culture within a learning organization. Obstacles are dealt with in a collaborative manner when a problem-solving spirit exists and there are expectations of ongoing learning, professionalism, and improvement (Ackerman, Donaldson, and Bogert 1996). Professional development has the power to increase collaboration between teachers to the point that expertise is built within the environment rather than exclusively looking outside the school for consultants to import their knowledge. Consultants can present information but they should also be involved in ongoing follow-up. The professional development program needs to have expertise accessible through the initial presenters or thoroughly trained staff who keep the effort moving positively. Easily accessed support eliminates the sense that the adaptation is impossible, which commonly arises when no overt support is given.

Implemented activities should connect individual renewal with the renewal of the entire school by emphasizing the importance of learning from one another as a cohesive unit. Rigorous standards are promoted to a great degree when a faculty functions as an example of a learning community. Since most teachers are accustomed to the isolation of self-contained classrooms, the educational impact without collaboration is often limited to a single class. Through a collaborative culture, the ideas, progress, and innovations of individual teachers can have an impact on an entire school population.

> **When an entire faculty is involved in an innovation, the transfer rate of training into classroom practice approaches 100 percent, whereas it is lower when only a part of the faculty is trained (Joyce and Showers 1995).**

The collaborative culture needs to include all teachers, not just a few. When an entire faculty is involved in an innovation, the transfer rate of training into classroom practice approaches 100 percent, whereas it is lower when only a part of the faculty is trained (Joyce and Showers 1995). Students, teachers, parents, and administrators need to feel a sense of ownership. The collaborative effort must be celebrated and clearly articulated by all site and district leaders in a way that the ideals and goals are not a surprise to anyone because they are part of the culture.

Adaptable to Change

Since the goals are clear and the staff understands the importance of collaboration, it is easier to tackle problems facing the school. The solutions to these problems naturally become the subjects of professional development. If the staff is not congenial to change, then the new strategies presented might not be implemented appropriately.

During the change process, both training and practice have to reside comfortably in the school setting. Training and practice are intensely collaborative activities where people depend on one another in a serious way during the early stages because they are putting into practice unfamiliar skills and knowledge. The study of teaching and curriculum becomes public, decisions become collective and more complicated, and connections between teachers and administrators become closer and reciprocal. Open discussion of areas needing improvement tends to cause temporary discomfort until the benefits of the change effort are obvious to the staff and become part of the normal routine.

Interestingly, as implementation of new ideas occurs, "learners often discover what they need to be effective," spurring further growth (Hawley and Valli 1999, 141). This helps the ongoing learning process because the growth and maturation of staff can be noticed. People share what they learn with others and do things differently based on what they learn. As some teachers grow, others who perhaps do not exhibit the same growth can feel left behind. Such growth can also cause anxiety if an overall sense of purpose behind the program is lacking, especially when the intent to engage all teachers is unclear. A shared understanding of purpose can assuage the vulnerability resulting from exposure of weaknesses within the school and remind all of the direction the school is taking to remedy the weaknesses.

Shared Understanding of Purpose

If the reasoning behind new strategies is not clear, then staff may not feel their effort is worthwhile. The professional development effort may feel forced and unnecessary unless the purpose is clear. As Fullan (Fullan 1982; Fullan and Stiegelbauer 1991) has pointed out, an innovation cannot be sustained unless there is a shared understanding of its purposes, rationale, and processes. The environment must be supportive.

The introduction of new concepts causes a period of cognitive conflict and disequilibrium. In this challenging period, the adult learner is likely to feel anxiety and frustration. If anxiety and frustration are overwhelming, the learner will not be able to resolve the conflict but will retreat to the stability of old assumptions and patterns of thinking. Rather than learning, a teacher in this situation might become rigidly entrenched in comfortable old ways of thinking.

> **If anxiety and frustration are overwhelming, the learner will not be able to resolve the conflict but will retreat to the stability of old assumptions and patterns of thinking.**

Shared understanding of purpose supplies the rationale behind the professional development program. If all understand the intent, student outcomes should be well defined. If practitioners begin implementation knowing what the results should be, the sense of whether they have taken the right direction will be both noticeable and the subject of dialogue with other practitioners.

CONSIDERATIONS ADDRESSED BY SUCCESSFUL PROFESSIONAL DEVELOPMENT PROGRAMS

1. Is there a team or core group of teachers who meets with the site administrator to give input on various matters? What are some ways such collaboration could be established for professional development purposes?
2. Are there any respected educators in the district or local area who could help with training efforts? If teachers are trained by someone they respect for his or her expertise, they are more likely to buy in to their feedback.
3. How can the professional development program help teachers assist their most difficult students?

Chapter Four

Emphasis on Teachers as Reflective Practitioners

Teachers must be viewed as professionals whose practice is constantly refined as the needs of the student population shift. Professional development has been defined as a continuous and incremental process built on the existing skills of practitioners (Holly 1991). Once student and teacher needs are analyzed and training is implemented, the larger burden on school leaders is to ensure the practice of new strategies. Sufficient time and follow-up to support mastery of new strategies and integration into practice is essential.

Sufficient time and follow-up to support mastery of new strategies and integration into practice is essential.

To motivate teacher participation, a strong connection between current teacher and student needs and the focus of the professional development effort should clarify the potential benefits to be gained through participation. Teachers with a high sense of efficacy tend to be part of projects that place heavy emphasis on professional development and teacher participation. A sense of efficacy is defined as "a belief that the teacher can help even the most difficult or unmotivated students" (McLaughlin 1991, 67). Other researchers agree that the most relevant rewards are derived from the belief that teachers would grow professionally and their students would benefit (Holly 1991; Lieberman and Miller 1991; McLaughlin 1991). In other words, teachers need to feel they can better assist their students through innovation and must be supported as practitioners to maximize student success and personal accomplishment.

Teachers need to feel they can better assist their students through innovation and must be supported as practitioners to maximize student success and personal accomplishment.

 Practical ongoing support methods need to be embedded into the school culture to combat the previous norm of isolation. Isolation is the enemy of improvement when the practitioner must be ready to meet constantly changing student needs. The sharing of expertise through dialogue needs to be embedded into the system as new strategies are implemented. Teachers need to be provided with regular "opportunities to explore, question, and debate to integrate new ideas into their repertoires and their classroom practice" (Danielson and McGreal 2000).

Isolation is the enemy of improvement when the practitioner must be ready to meet constantly changing student needs.

Development is promoted by reflection on new techniques. Regular, systematic reflection supports individuals in confronting old assumptions and methods. As old assumptions about teaching conflict with new student needs, teachers realize the need to approach teaching as problem solving. A culture where teachers have opportunities to dialogue gives practitioners the space they need to refine their own experiences and view each lesson as a problem-solving exercise rather than a roadblock.

The gap between the initial development of a skill and the practice of the skill until it becomes part of a teacher's repertoire can be filled by observation and dialogue. This mutually beneficial relationship between colleagues incorporates not only classroom observations but shared efforts of planning together, developing support materials, and pooling experience through dialogue.

This mutually beneficial relationship between colleagues incorporates not only classroom observations but shared efforts of planning together, developing support materials, and pooling experience through dialogue.

Teachers are classroom professionals who refine their practice each day. To enhance their practice, school leaders must create a climate where there is trust among practitioners as they observe one another. Observations and ensuing dialogue exist to refine skills and solve problems. There is no room for destructive criticism if the intent is to support growth in an atmosphere of trust, as new techniques are refined to meet the needs of the current student population. The teacher can actively participate by helping plan when observations take place, rather than simply becoming an object to be observed, and can determine what aspects of the class are important for the observer to note.

Positive effects of observation and dialogue hold true for increased learning among veteran and new practitioners. New teachers in a mentoring program involving peer observations are more likely to remain in the teaching profession beyond four years; teachers not involved in this type of observation process do not remain in the profession as long (Odell and Ferraro 1992). Teachers involved in a peer observation project in Washington indicated they were less anxious and more comfortable when observed by another teacher rather than by an administrator. The teachers desired more feedback, felt the observations were helpful in improving their teaching skills, and desired the opportunity to observe other classes (Munson 1998).

Teachers indicated they were less anxious and more comfortable when observed by another teacher rather than by an administrator.

The professional development program needs to be operated as a large-scale action research project and improved continually as staff members assess its impact. The burgeoning professional community then recognizes that they have the ability and obligation to reconnoiter based on discoveries as implementation occurs. The obligation and ability to adjust the program is clarified through regular reflective dialogue, feedback on progress the staff has made as a whole, examination of student work samples, and reviews of support practices. The ongoing support practices therefore inform the change process.

CONSIDERATIONS ADDRESSED BY SUCCESSFUL
PROFESSIONAL DEVELOPMENT PROGRAMS

1. Is your school one of isolation or collaboration? If collaboration occurs, how often does it occur and in what format?
2. Do your teachers need training in reflective practice where each lesson
   or review of work samples is viewed as a problem-solving exercise to
   improve practice?
3. Have any teachers on your staff served as peer coaches in some way?
   Can their expertise be tapped to provide a format for teachers to use
   when observing one another, planning/dialoguing, or developing support materials together?

Chapter Five

Peer Observation

The clear majority of teachers in my study felt that peer observation is a beneficial professional development strategy and that they would like more observation opportunities to enhance their own practice. Teachers need confirmation that the way they are currently teaching their program is correct. This section describes why this strategy is beneficial and why most teachers have not been able to participate in the activity.

PEER OBSERVATION IS BENEFICIAL

Eighty-one percent of the teachers in the study said that peer observations are beneficial and that such observations enhance overall professional development because teachers can see the new strategies practiced in actual classrooms. Within self-contained teaching environments, these opportunities are typically given to new rather than experienced teachers, even though all need to observe and grow professionally. Teachers feel a need for depth in training that reading a manual or sitting in a meeting does not provide. According to the data, observing a whole lesson in realistic conditions provides the necessary learning conditions all teachers need.

Peer observation marks a departure from the independent world of the self-contained, nonprescriptive classroom environment. Through peer observation, teachers can get ideas from teachers who are doing things differently.

> **Peer observations provide valid points of reference since students from that community are directly taught rather than students from another area in a video or training seminar.**

Teachers perceived peer observation as a means of detailed support not found in typical training. Peer observations provide valid points of reference since students from that community are directly taught rather than students from another area in a video or training seminar. Sixty-three percent of the teachers in the study stressed that initial training was not only overwhelming in scope but didn't give a clear picture of what the teaching would look like. Teachers described video footage of four or five students working with one teacher at a time—but remarked that unlikely scenarios in training sessions do not provide specific, applicable information. Teachers were at times grouped to participate as students in classroom simulations but teachers indicated this was never for a significant length of time or in realistic conditions of twenty or more students in a classroom situation. Teachers felt what was missing was an observational, realistic learning environment.

Many teachers, although not involved in peer observations, perceived observations of actual practice as exposing the viewer to a clear picture of what they will be doing, whereas listening to a trainer or reading a manual is not concrete enough. Teacher Lori Clapper stated,

> After initial training it would be nice to watch an expert [demonstrate a few lessons]. . . . A teaching classroom experience would be much more beneficial if it was actually done with them doing it with a class of children so you can watch all the components being done. And to me there would be no questions. But this is all very superficial because it's all abstract. This is what you do and some modeling is done but with adults pretending to be children sometimes it's not the same, it's just not the same.

> **Even experienced teachers need to know they are on the right track.**

Over half the teachers in my study felt observing actual practice can confirm what experienced teachers already know. Even experienced teachers need to know they are on the right track. Experienced second-grade teacher Rick Czarapata commented on having a new teacher observe him: "Well I got a lot of praise from this individual. And I was thinking that to myself, that's nice to hear, but I'm not one hundred percent sure whether or not I'm doing this correctly."

Experienced as well as new teachers can pick up ideas and benefit from simple validation of their teaching practices. Seventy percent agreed that experienced teachers do not typically have the opportunity to observe other teachers. Rather, they are asked to model for others. Repeatedly, teachers voiced the potential benefits of peer observation opportunities for new and experienced teachers.

Experienced teachers gain ideas by observing other classrooms. An experienced third-grade teacher who observed an experienced teacher's classroom at another site described how the experience was beneficial:

> I got some papers that they used, handouts for writing meaningful sentences and cute web ideas. . . . I learned classroom management ideas on how to organize various activities, moving kids around, and that sort of thing. I enjoyed seeing others doing some things the same as I did them. That made me feel more confident in what I was doing.

I enjoyed seeing others doing some things the same as I did them.

Peer observation is perceived as a necessary, beneficial tool that is not consistently available to all teachers.

COMFORT LEVELS AND TRUST AS OBSTACLES

Comfort levels and trust among staff are obstacles inhibiting the practice of peer observation.

Comfort levels are affected when teachers sense they are "imposing" by asking another teacher to observe. Teachers who attempt to arrange coverage of their own classes may sense discomfort in that they may feel they are imposing on busy administrators or others to do them this "favor." It is not part of most school cultures for teachers to have regular release time. Someone with suitable credentials who is not responsible for the supervision of a class of children needs to take the place of the teacher for liability reasons. For example, an administrator could personally cover a first-grade teacher's class so he or she could observe a math lesson in another first-grade class. However, administrators or other faculty members who do not have direct responsibility for a set group of children are typically too busy with their own work to release teachers on a regular basis for observation purposes. Most teachers would not want to impose on others, even for such a worthwhile purpose. A few teachers expressed feeling a violation of space when someone is in their classroom since it is customarily the individual teacher's domain. In other words, the feeling is one of having a visitor at home seeing the common family interactions that are normally considered private. Classrooms are often so closed to outsiders that there could be a sense of intrusion whenever there is a visitor.

One elementary teacher sees the benefits as well as the comfort level issue when she describes peer observation as "a very beneficial thing. I do foresee, though, some teachers not being happy with it, seeing it as an intrusion on their little domain." Several teachers pointed out the "domain" of the self-contained classroom is part of most school cultures. If no one has ever been allowed to observe another teacher, discomfort may result from this new, unique opportunity.

Based on my personal experience as a teacher and administrator, isolation is common within the school environment; having someone in a classroom to watch a teacher interact with students is typically the sole domain of administrators.

The majority of teachers felt that the tensions that might be created through observations could be assuaged to some extent with administrative support. Debbie Johnson stated, "I feel like I'm imposing on that teacher. Whereas if it's arranged by administration you know it's just . . . that's the way it is. . . . When we're observed it's a little uncomfortable whether it's one of your peers or not. So I have a hard time saying, 'Can I come in and watch you?' You know it's an imposition." Teachers sense that if the school provides someone to regularly provide release time to the teachers to observe others, those who take advantage of this opportunity will not be perceived as imposing.

The issue of trust arises because teachers feel "on the spot" when someone is in the room.

The issue of trust arises because teachers feel "on the spot" when someone is in the room. Anxiety over "maybe somebody's going to come in and watch you and you're going to do the wrong thing" is an issue that arose regarding peer observation. Observation time is viewed as a time to "pick things up" on your own but could pose difficulty since teachers, as elementary teacher Carlos Sevilla described, may feel you are there to "criticize or . . . pick up something and come running back to the lounge." In other words, the fear of a hidden agenda arises when the intention of the practice is unclear and not incorporated into the everyday school culture.

Yet the need and desire for peer observation is clear since several teachers in the study had observed on their own personal, unpaid time. Several teachers of three-track year-round schools had opted to observe teachers during their off-track time while other tracks of classes are still in session, in order to minimize inconvenience regarding classroom coverage. This way, the teacher can "devote [his or her] time and not worry about it and just listen," according to Maria Ana Camarena.

> **If you want to hit home runs you go to the park or the batting cage and you practice. I come in and sit in the back corner and I just watch.**

Carlos Sevilla compared observations during his off-track time to baseball practice: "If you want to hit home runs you go to the park or the batting cage and you practice. I come in and sit in the back corner and I just watch her, I take notes . . . don't interrupt her, and when the class is over she's more than willing to answer any questions or make suggestions or give advice." It is appropriate to conclude that peer observation is a useful teaching tool since some teachers who want to enhance their practice willingly donate unpaid time for this purpose.

Once the innovation of peer observation is established as part of the school culture, the problems of discomfort and trust may give way to great benefits since teachers could see the innovation as beneficial for practice as well as camaraderie. First- and second-grade teacher Matthew Bootz sees the self-esteem benefits: "It's great for camaraderie, I believe. You lift up the spirits of each other. If you do something great and somebody else wants to borrow it from you, you know you've done something great. It's a compliment . . . consistency for the students." Self-esteem is raised for both the observer and the observed. A minority of teachers expressed thoughts regarding the empowerment of the observer to improve by implementing the most meaningful observed techniques.

To make this innovation a regular part of a school's culture, there must be someone prepared to take on the responsibility of relieving teachers for the purpose of observing others. While an individual in this position is a rare commodity, any time spent by such a person would be an incredibly useful part of an adaptation to a new culture of ongoing learning. Were it offered consistently and made a regular part of the school environment, more teachers would use peer observation as a learning tool.

> **Were it offered consistently and made a regular part of the school environment, more teachers would use peer observation as a learning tool.**

Incorporating peer observation into the school culture could mark a shift to a more professional environment for teachers. Teacher David Gaynor summarized the similar thoughts of many teachers: "We are supposed to be professionals, and if you are, you want to continue to grow and the way to do that is [observe]. . . . When you're self-contained, you're kind of an island. You're an island in this sea and you have your classroom and that's really about it. Any opportunity you have to step outside of your little box . . . " Once teachers step out of their isolated classroom, they would likely benefit from reflection and dialogue.

> **We are supposed to be professionals, and if you are, you want to continue to grow and the way to do that is [observe].**

CONSIDERATIONS ADDRESSED BY SUCCESSFUL PROFESSIONAL DEVELOPMENT PROGRAMS

1. Which teachers could be approached to observe a colleague so they in turn could speak about the experience to staff at a meeting when this professional development activity is introduced?

2. Would peer observation at your site best be used to focus on how to work with a particular group of students (e.g., low socioeconomic, English learners, etc.)?
3. What system can be established to ensure coverage of the observing teacher?
4. How will the nonevaluative, confidential nature of this practice be preserved?

Chapter Six

Reflective Dialogue

All the teachers in the study felt that opportunities for reflective dialogue would enhance professional learning. Why are these opportunities so rare for teachers? In what way are reflection and dialogue opportunities useful? These questions are explored through the following themes: rare opportunities, venting and problem solving, and building camaraderie.

RARE OPPORTUNITIES

Seventy-eight percent of the teachers in the study felt that opportunities for reflection and dialogue are rare.

Teachers revealed there is no regularly scheduled time for reflection and dialogue because meetings are overstructured and announcement driven.

Teachers revealed there is no regularly scheduled time for reflection and dialogue because meetings are overstructured and announcement driven. During this study, meetings were observed where the entire staff was in attendance at once or grouped by ability of students they serve. These meetings were agenda driven and led by an administrator who did not often provide opportunities for staff to interact because time was usually not allotted for this purpose. The agenda typically featured new items to discuss. Some teachers described such meetings as times where administrators talk to the staff rather than lead discussions.

Since reflection and dialogue are not embedded practices at most schools, attempts to foster these rare opportunities are usually viewed by administrators as unnecessarily dragging out the meeting. Agendas hold off open discussion time until the end of the meeting under the agenda heading "other." According to teachers, because of time constraints, those who raise "other" issues are viewed as lengthening the meeting. Teachers have the feeling that they are rushed by the end of the meeting, either to get to their classrooms in the morning or to leave after school, even when they have the opportunity to raise important issues.

Since opportunities for reflection and dialogue are so rare, teachers seize opportunities informally when possible.

Since opportunities for reflection and dialogue are so rare, teachers seize opportunities informally when possible. The year-round track system employed by the schools in this study allowed teachers to informally seek out these rare opportunities for dialogue and reflection among teachers on a different track. The year-round calendar is one in which vacations are taken throughout the year on a rotating basis rather than in one unified, longer summer break. Since one track is always on vacation, the track returning to school can "catch up" with those who have pushed ahead through the curriculum. Teachers liked the chance to question and "pick the brain" of teachers who had been on track while they were off and had progressed further into the program. The schedule caused many teachers to take advantage of dialoguing opportunities when teachers were on campus a day or so prior to their particular group of students returning from being off track.

Dialogue opportunities arising from tracks of students and teachers departing for vacation while some were returning from vacation was an unexpected benefit of this type of schedule. However, a minority of teachers in this study also referred to several disadvantages of this type of calendar. On a traditional calendar, all teachers and students would have been going through the program at the same pace without one or two particular groups moving ahead. This benefit of some teachers progressing further ahead of other teachers in the program prompted a fourth-grade teacher to reflect on the need to dialogue.

They started when we were off track . . . [and when we were coming back after a vacation]. We picked their brain . . . and got a lot of really good ideas. And we didn't have to make the same mistakes, now we made other ones but those particular ones we didn't make. We need more time than they give us to talk with each other. I have about ten questions I'd still like to sit down and ask and get feedback but it just doesn't happen.

> **We picked their brain . . . and got a lot of really good ideas. And we didn't have to make the same mistakes.**

Because teachers recognize the need for this type of interaction, they found a way to enhance their learning regardless of obstacles they encountered.

VENTING AND PROBLEM SOLVING

Fifty-nine percent of the teachers referred to the need to vent frustrations as well as solve problems. Referring to the need to vent while overcoming obstacles, fourth-grade teacher Patricia Nunley viewed the weekly articulation meetings as a strength because the "frustration level only goes so high . . . and then someone else [says] 'Well, what I've tried with this is . . .' and then you go 'Oh, I'm going to try that next time.'" Dialogue shows teachers that potential obstacles may be positives. Lisa Anderson described, "[The person providing feedback] tried to be very positive in finding ways around things that I saw as roadblocks."

> **The frustration level only goes so high . . . and then someone else [says] "Well, what I've tried with this is . . ." and then you go "Oh, I'm going to try that next time."**

Some teachers feel uncomfortable with dialogue because they do not want to bring up negatives or problems in front of administrators. Administrators often tend toward a positive attitude about the professional development focus without as much focus on problematic areas. A former elementary teacher commented: "People don't want to bring up the negatives but then . . . every time you bring up a negative it's because you're having problems or you're struggling with something. . . . Someone might say, 'Oh, have you tried this?'" For a minority of teachers, the meetings do not accomplish much because dialogue is not as open or useful as it could be.

> **It is useful to group teachers by their students' ability levels for dialogue purposes.**

When a whole staff meets together to dialogue, the ideas shared may not consistently apply to all present. A few teachers mentioned that since dialogue and reflection often lead to problem-solving exercises, it is useful to group teachers by their students' ability levels for dialogue purposes. Based on input from the focus groups, if teachers exchange students during the school day by ability level, traditional grade-level meetings may not be the best use of time. Some teachers work with academically advanced students and perhaps could not contribute much to a discussion with teachers of lower-level students. Jane Heyman recognized that grouping teachers for dialogue purposes by student ability level is "helpful because we're with our particular group. . . . The afternoon can be a free-for-all." The "afternoon" refers to meetings by grade level where teachers do not necessarily serve similar students and therefore might feel that meeting together is a waste of time.

A few teachers recalled a discussion of ability grouping in the staff lounge. Teachers had compared memories of self-contained classrooms versus the merits of trading students for grouping purposes. One teacher recalled that she spoke about discomfort with three or four distinct reading groups in her class when she felt a teacher can only really focus on one group at a time. The other teachers in the discussion agreed that the various reading groups were not directly interacting with the teacher and instead were involved in individualized assignments that they could already do. Reflection ensued on how whole-group instruction could potentially have more impact on a larger number of students than small-group instruction in a self-contained classroom.

Fifty-six percent of the teachers in my study recognized that reflection and dialogue cannot solely happen in the staff lounge but need to be incorporated into the regular school environment.

BUILDING CAMARADERIE

Fifty-nine percent of the teachers participating in the study perceived time for dialogue and reflection as time for building camaraderie among staff members. The data reflect that teachers who exchange ideas feel they are supporting one another and able to access the support they need.

You can't schedule the problem into the agenda.

In a dynamic environment where there is purposeful conversation regarding professional practice, a bond is built that is greater than the single efforts of any individual. Yet this synergy needs to originate in a trusting environment. A fourth-grade teacher stated, "You can't schedule the problem into the agenda. . . . They're going to ask the person next door, their peer group." If a teacher senses a safe environment and can go to peers for input, there is a great sense of trust. Once trust is part of daily life within a school to help teachers deal with day-to-day stress, the larger problems can be dealt with in an easier manner since all are accustomed to discussing the issues and supporting one another through change. Matthew Bootz described the synergy that can come from regular, purposeful dialogue: "When you have the larger [issues to discuss], those people who have made a bond [through dialogue can] pass that positive on to other people, if for instance a program is accepted or not accepted."

Almost all the teachers in the study recognized that regular dialogue within the school day shows that the school values this practice. Teachers cite the need to often spend their own time preparing materials and reviewing curriculum. Dialogue would lessen time spent in isolated preparation. Debbie Johnson feels that to ease the incorporation of new ideas, many teachers need "more time to help figure out how we're going to implement any staff development idea. Sometimes we're really given good ideas but then you have to go home and spend five hours reading a manual and . . . three hours figuring out lessons." This quote speaks to the idea of following through on professional development within the school day. According to teachers, a topic must be relatively unimportant if dialogue, reflection, and overall development of implementation ideas are not a structured part of the environment. If it were important to the school, it would be discussed during the school day.

> **If it were important to the school, it would be discussed during the school day.**

For example, two teachers mentioned recent training in an art program. They felt if they had been given structured time after initial training in which they could work purposefully on the incorporation of the new program, there would have been much more incorporation of the new ideas. Since the organization was not emphasizing the program's importance by ensuring teacher dialogue, implementation was dependent on the individual drive of the teacher.

> **The incorporation of time for dialogue and reflection into the school day is "almost like getting a bonus."**

The incorporation of time for dialogue and reflection into the school day is so rare that the feelings of many teachers are summarized in Carlos Sevilla's quote regarding release time to collaborate with peers: "It's almost like getting a bonus." This teacher was referring to a structured release time that was provided once a week where teachers could collaborate regarding curricular issues. Most teachers feel like more opportunities should be created for purposes of dialogue and reflection.

CONSIDERATIONS ADDRESSED BY SUCCESSFUL PROFESSIONAL DEVELOPMENT PROGRAMS

1. How could meetings at your site include beneficial opportunities for reflection and dialogue?
2. How should teachers be grouped for dialogue purposes: by ability level, grade level, or other configuration/grouping?
3. What collaborative practices are currently valued at your site? Would an ongoing collaborative model be a huge shift at your site?

Chapter Seven

Feedback

Fifty-two percent of the teachers in this study viewed constructive feedback from an experienced practitioner as an asset to their professional development. Feedback that is knowledge-based, consistent, authentic, and direct is respected and requested.

VOICES OF EXPERIENCE

Teachers respect feedback from experts trained in a program or particular teaching strategy. Through feedback, they express their breadth of knowledge and experience. Teachers want practical suggestions directly related to the programs they are teaching rather than vague platitudes or criticisms they might receive from administrators who are not intensely familiar with a particular program or teaching strategy. Teachers desire specific "next steps" and recognize when such recommendations are coming from someone who is familiar with the details of the program.

> **Teachers want practical suggestions directly related to the programs they are teaching rather than vague platitudes or criticisms they might receive from administrators who are not intensely familiar with a particular program or teaching strategy.**

Teachers in this study had the benefit of visits from specialists in their area of focus. When the specialists arrived to observe teachers in this study, there was immediate recognition of their experience by the quality of their feedback. The insights they shared were based on a brief visit to each classroom.

Prompt feedback with topics still fresh in the minds of teachers is ideal. Teachers recognize that the specialists commented on what they saw during that one day and not based on exhaustive observations. Feedback that is specific, makes sense, and helps guide the teacher, especially when it is only based on a brief visit, is appreciated. Teachers recognized the observers as experts who did not give out vague opinions or platitudes.

Teachers feel the experience-based knowledge of those visiting classrooms is immediately recognizable in the highly detailed quality of feedback received. Curriculum expert and former elementary classroom teacher Linda Jaramillo felt it would be advantageous to have an expert observer visit to give feedback on the area of focus "and be there on call until the experience was built in." By extension, any significant focus area of teacher professional development needs to have an expert provide feedback rather than evaluation-driven criticism.

A small number of teachers expressed concern about feedback that does not come from an expert in the area of focus. Genuine feedback is unclouded with administrative or political issues. At times, administrative feedback can feel threatening to teachers and therefore be regarded as less genuine.

The motivation of the effort must be altruistic and not linked to evaluation. A fourth-grade teacher noted the importance of the individual's expertise: "[The specialist] keyed in on [all these qualities that] didn't concern [typical administrators] at all. [Her feedback pertained to] her program but we didn't feel threatened." The teacher was referring to details administrators must consider when providing feedback to teachers, such as paperwork, promptness, maintenance, and safety concerns, in addition to curricular details such as providing the basis of a postobservation teacher conference. Teachers need practice-related feedback to enhance the choices they make in the classroom.

It was clear to the majority of teachers that the specialists focused on how to implement the program correctly and got their feedback across in a nonthreatening manner. Carlos Sevilla described how he received helpful feedback.

They'll make suggestions so you know the suggestions are covering your weaknesses. [For example], I didn't really catch your two-minute edit. You should try it this way. And then I think they're doing it so that we can say, you know that's one of my weak points, I need a little help there. And they're right there. It's almost like they roll out suggestions. Try this, this, and that. They come in and they pick up on your positive, on your strengths, and then they'll make a suggestion and listen to what you have to say.

It's almost like they roll out suggestions.

All teachers in the study recognized the observers as concerned with practical application of ideas rather than platitudes. When considering the importance of feedback from experts, Jane Heyman mentioned: "It was very helpful in that strategies [were presented]. . . . It wasn't critical at all."

It wasn't critical at all.

The source of feedback is important to teachers because experience matters. Teachers repeatedly mentioned how out-of-the-classroom staff members on site have not taught the new, specific curriculum in the classroom and, as fourth-grade teacher Kimberly Wright stated, "actually implementing it in the classroom is a whole different thing." The desire for knowledgeable feedback opened up a valid concern expressed by Debbie Johnson regarding the comparison of administrators and specialists.

I think, actually being in the classroom, I would think the administrator would know less than we do. . . . I think it would be from knowledge more than anything else. If the administrator knew as much as [the specialist] does, amen, that's fine. But this gal knows what she's talking about. And she can zoom in on all the places where we are stumbling and help us along and give us a nudge in the right direction."

But this gal knows what she's talking about. And she can zoom in on all the places where we are stumbling and help us along and give us a nudge in the right direction.

Almost all teachers want the source of their feedback to be knowledge-able and concerned with practice. Teachers repeatedly spoke to the need for feedback that is consistent, authentic, and direct.

CONSISTENT, AUTHENTIC, AND DIRECT FEEDBACK

Experienced and inexperienced teachers in the study desired consistent, authentic, and direct feedback. Consistent feedback is wanted because teachers are concerned with growth but do not want a huge list of areas where they need to improve. Like students, teachers need to work in steps on specific areas and receive experienced input before moving on. This can beneficially occur when experienced eyes are there to check up on teacher progress at regular intervals.

> **Like students, teachers need to work in steps on specific areas and receive experienced input before moving on. This can bene-ficially occur when experienced eyes are there to check up on teacher progress at regular intervals.**

The specialists/observers in this study maintained consistency. They provided incremental feedback during briefings, after a day of observa-tions, giving teachers "next steps" to work on and allowing for clarifica-tion of ideas or concerns. Regarding consistency and reliability of incre-mental feedback, fourth-grade teacher Kimberly Wright commented, "They come back and give you little suggestions this time. Then the next visit, they'll suggest working on something else. This way you are not overwhelmed, even when they're observing your classroom. Next time I'm sure they'll have another suggestion just to help us iron out the kinks."

> **They come back and give you little suggestions this time. Then the next visit, they'll suggest working on something else. This way you are not overwhelmed, even when they're observing your classroom. Next time I'm sure they'll have another suggestion just to help us iron out the kinks.**

Nineteen percent mentioned the tendency of the site facilitator and administrators to visit classes taught by new teachers with more frequency. This takes potential opportunities away from experienced teachers to receive feedback, since only so much time can be spent in this manner by administration. Experienced teachers feel, although they are likely teaching the program well, they would still like feedback. Interestingly, they are even cognizant of indirect methods the school could employ to know whether or not they are on task. For example, experienced teachers recognized that supply check-out sheets could be reviewed to see who is borrowing particular materials to assess which teachers are keeping up with the pace of the program. Experienced teachers recognize they are not growing professionally to the fullest possible extent due to inconsistent feedback.

These seldom-visited teachers may have doubts about their implementation of new curriculum and would like feedback to confirm that what they are doing is correct. Maria Ana Camarena stated, "Once you have the training, you need time to [practice it] and then you need . . . another follow-up so that you get reassured." Without feedback it is possible for even experienced teachers to, as Lisa Anderson described, "continue to do something incorrectly, [making it] hard to go back once you've gotten in a pattern of doing it wrong."

> **Without feedback it is possible for even experienced teachers to "continue to do something incorrectly, [making it] hard to go back once you've gotten in a pattern of doing it wrong."**

A question of feedback artificiality arose since teachers are often told what the specialists will look for in advance of the visits. Third-grade teacher Lisa Fowler felt "if they would've just went out to the rooms it would have been more . . . authentic," since teachers would have been observed going through their daily routine.

Kindergarten teacher Lori Clapper succinctly puts the reasoning behind the need for feedback in an authentic, everyday setting.

I like the feedback personally. . . . It's an opportunity for me to learn. And you know a lot of times it's a positive, it might be, it doesn't have to necessarily be a negative, but they might say, "Have you ever tried doing it this way?" And to me that's an opportunity to grow as a teacher and when you don't have people coming in and you're just observed three times during the year every other year . . . it's really difficult because in your mind it's so introspective, you think you're doing it but you don't have the opportunity to step out or get the feedback to see if you are reaching all those children, or if you are really doing a good job teaching. I welcome feedback and having people come in and observe me. That's the way I look at it.

I like the feedback personally. . . . It's an opportunity for me to learn.

↙ Direct feedback is not supplied if this practice is not a regular part of the school culture. Experienced staff members who can provide consistent, authentic, and direct feedback are necessities to a school applying a new innovation or sharpening skills in a specific area. The feedback must be part of the school climate and practice-oriented.

CONSIDERATIONS ADDRESSED BY SUCCESSFUL PROFESSIONAL DEVELOPMENT PROGRAMS

1. How often do teachers at your site receive feedback? From whom?
2. Is there a resident expert at your site or within your school district who could provide direct feedback to teachers in a particular area or focus?
3. Could a professor from a local university be approached about regularly consulting for professional development purposes?
4. What types of goals/objectives are set annually for teachers and the site at large? Who writes them and how are they measured?

Chapter Eight

How to Improve Teacher Learning Environments

An enormous shift from isolation to ongoing, collaborative professional development must occur in the culture of our schools. This move from traditional isolation must be aligned with a specific schoolwide focus and needs to incorporate peer observation, consistent feedback, and reflective dialogue.

✦ CULTURAL SHIFT

The majority of teachers in this study were ready for this shift to a culture of ongoing learning and would like to see the strategies enacted at their school sites.

> **During focus groups, teachers named a variety of obstacles that must be overcome to create a culture of ongoing professional development: isolation, lack of time for reflection and dialogue, availability of support personnel for such things as release time or feedback, and accountability concerns regarding unmonitored professional activities.**

It is crucial to note the current impediments to a huge shift in school culture toward ongoing professional development. During focus groups, teachers named a variety of obstacles that must be overcome to create a culture of ongoing professional development: isolation, lack of time for reflection and dialogue, availability of support personnel for such things

as release time or feedback, and accountability concerns regarding un-
monitored professional activities.

Table 8.1 outlines these impediments to the necessary cultural shift and
shows possible ways of remedying these obstacles during a movement
away from the status quo. The recommendations pertaining to each remedy are enumerated here and discussed in chapter 9.

The fourteen recommendations found in the following chapter directly link to the focus-group findings. For example, concerning peer
observation, Debbie Johnson stated, "I feel like I'm imposing on that
teacher. Whereas if it's arranged by administration . . . that's the way it
is." This teacher felt discomfort would no longer be an issue if peer observations were part of the school culture. It is not as simple as solely
having the administration tell everyone that peer observations are
mandatory. There needs to be a clarification of why peer observations
should be part of the culture and a structure in place to ensure the details
are taken care of.

> **One of the issues working against a culture of ongoing profes-
> sional development: optional information only accessible to a few
> does not engage an entire staff.**

Many innovative professional development programs, projects, and efforts offer professional development support to teachers on a voluntary
basis. However, therein lies one of the issues working against a culture of
ongoing professional development: optional information only accessible
to a few does not engage an entire staff (Darling-Hammond and
McLaughlin 1999). Although usually successful, mentor programs tend to
assist inexperienced teachers or those designated as in need of help. This
study demands a movement toward a culture of ongoing professional development that involves *every* staff member.

Movement toward a culture of ongoing professional development begins with a shared schoolwide focus. The mutually agreed upon schoolwide focus drives ongoing learning. Professional learning occurs not
just for the sake of taking in new information but to enhance student
learning in connection to the benchmark goals set within the well-
defined focus.

Table 8.1. Impediments and Remedies to Cultural Shifts

Professional Development Strategy	Impediment to Cultural Shift	Remedy	Recommendations
Peer observation; dialogue	Isolation	Cultural shift: Classroom visitations and discussions of everyday teaching practice are the norm.	4, 12, 14
Reflective dialogue	Lack of time; agenda driven by administrative rather than instructional concerns.	Cultural shift: Regular time set aside to involve all teachers in reflection and dialogue—not viewed as only to be done voluntarily if there is "extra time."	6, 7, 8, 9, 14
Peer observation; feedback	Lack of out-of-classroom staff to provide support; insufficient time for administrators or others to observe and give feedback to experienced and new teachers alike; no structure ensuring release time.	Cultural shift: Create teacher support position on staff—a knowledgeable out-of-classroom teacher would provide feedback and release time to experienced and new teachers alike; in addition, administration and all others available provide regular feedback and set up a system to ensure all teachers have opportunities to observe.	5, 10, 11, 14
Reflective dialogue; peer observation; feedback	No clear means to monitor use of time by administration.	Cultural shift: Buy-in from teachers during creation of the professional development plan enhances the willingness for all to participate in ongoing activities; increased learning and camaraderie ensue if plan is realistic, valued, and followed; benchmarks provide deadlines to encourage direct connection to student learning.	1, 2, 3, 13, 14

SCHOOLWIDE FOCUS

Ongoing Support to Shared Commitment

Peer observation, consistent feedback, and reflective dialogue are perceived as beneficial for teacher learning and best provided when helping teachers work toward a specific schoolwide focus. Commitment to the schoolwide focus drives all aspects of the professional development program. When teachers see administrators actively monitoring and participating in the program, teacher receptivity to professional development activities is enhanced. The results of improvement efforts in the area of focus are tracked publicly when problematic issues are openly discussed and addressed. This openness to discuss problems reaffirms the shared responsibility of teachers and administrators to instructional improvement (Little 1999).

Teachers recalled that individual teachers had determined small-scale implementation of new strategies in the past, because there was often no schoolwide focus or simply no follow-up. During past reform programs, follow-up visits were not regularly held to see how the program was enacted. There was rarely a sign of visible, schoolwide commitment or concern for the manner in which the program was implemented.

The majority of teachers in the study perceived administrative and support staff as more readily available to assist teachers during implementation of the current program than during previous reform efforts. One teacher mentioned how she was struck by the fact that administrators were now regularly visiting classrooms. The classroom visits by administrators showed commitment to the program.

Yet visible commitment goes beyond interest by administrators. A second-grade teacher mentioned that "true commitment and follow-up must be shown by all staff and administration [by asking], 'Are the children improving?' 'Does [the new program] work?'" Teachers felt all staff members needed to explore all the questions and delve into suitable solutions to show the depth of commitment to the program.

Schools with a shared purpose have a collective energy and readiness to explore ways to resolve problems and curricular issues. The environment is galvanized, according to Matthew Bootz, "because everybody believes in the same thing, in the purpose of it, because once you have that, you're not going to have a problem with the program." This energy must be harnessed from the very beginning of the shift to a culture of ongoing professional development.

> **Schools with a shared purpose have a collective energy and readiness to explore ways to resolve problems and curricular issues.**

Fourth- and fifth-grade teacher Angel Cervantes commented on the importance of common goals in relation to school culture: "There's no point in having people come in and tell you 'do this' and 'do that' or 'fix this' or 'let's all get together and talk as a grade level' if there are no goals. . . . So it's not just meeting for the sake of meeting or discussing improvement for the sake of improvement. . . . We have a master plan." Without a shared focus, teachers might be inclined to view professional development strategies of peer observation, reflective dialogue, and consistent feedback as unwanted and unnecessary. However, a clear understanding of the "big picture" redirects energy when teachers are losing focus, reminding them of the ongoing professional development culture of the school.

Teachers in the study felt the shared commitment was due to a "big picture" all could see. This focus gives teachers a track to run on toward benchmark goals. Shared commitment by tying student progress to the professional development training helps teachers perceive the training activities as worthwhile.

Build Camaraderie by Working Together at the Same Pace

Teachers in the study consistently referred to the "self-contained classroom" element. The self-contained classroom was described as one where teachers work independently, interpreting curriculum differently while focused on the same general grade-level themes. Most feel that the varying interpretations of curriculum could lead to a sense of competition, with teachers feeling that some may do a better job than others. In such cases, the pacing can be dramatically different, leading teachers to feel they are taking too long to cover the same material or that they are not covering the information in depth.

The sense that some are further ahead of others in the curriculum causes feelings of inadequacy among some teachers. This inadequacy might arise when some teachers move faster with their students through some concepts than other teachers. The perception might be that all should ideally be at the same pace and some teachers might perceive one class being at a higher academic level simply because a teacher chose to spend a longer period of time on one concept. Fourth-grade teacher Patricia Nunley explained it this way: "It's not that whole thing where you think to yourself, 'that class is so much further ahead; we're taking way too much time on this.' It's not like that anymore. It's more personal . . . and that's definitely a benefit personally and professionally. It validates you."

Teachers felt specific, benchmark-type assessments motivate both teachers and students to focus on particular areas with a short-term goal in mind rather than the typical long-term goals of covering curriculum and doing well on state standardized tests.

Teachers say more camaraderie results from all teachers doing similar lessons at the same pace rather than the previously existing curiosity about what others are doing. Teachers repeatedly mentioned the idea of camaraderie, that all are "in the same boat." Teachers began learning the new innovation at the same time; dialogue regarding strategies and pacing ensued. This shift away from an independent, self-contained classroom atmosphere built camaraderie and lessened feelings of intimidation and competition.

A schoolwide focus bands teachers together. Dialogue, feedback, and other professional development aspects were logical to teachers in that they understood the purpose behind them. Camaraderie was created because all teachers were learning the program regardless of years of experience in teaching.

PEER OBSERVATION

Peer observation clearly inspired the most enthusiasm from teachers when compared to reflective dialogue and consistent feedback. Peer observations are perceived as beneficial in four ways:

- The activity can provide feedback that the observer is on the right track regarding the innovation, even if nothing particularly new is learned;

- The activity is learner driven since the observer picks up what is most meaningful on his or her own;
- The opportunity for further dialogue could be inspired by the activity because both the observer and the observed are engaged in a learning process;
- The experience can enhance the self-esteem of both parties in that the observed teacher feels the strategies presented are of value to others and the observer might be inspired to improve his or her own teaching through what was seen.

Impediments to this process include a climate of isolation whereby the observer would be intruding on others, the sense that it is inconvenient to obtain coverage for the teacher who would like to observe others, and the activity is primarily used for teachers who need assistance rather than all teachers regardless of skill level.

Teachers stated that their desire to observe peers often goes unfulfilled for various reasons. Impediments to this process include a climate of isolation whereby the observer would be intruding on others, the sense that it is inconvenient to obtain coverage for the teacher who would like to observe others, and the activity is primarily used for teachers who need assistance rather than all teachers regardless of skill level.

Isolation is common in most schools. A teacher might work next door to a peer for years and never see that person in practice. Administrators may visit on occasion, yet even their presence can evoke a sense that personal classroom space is violated in some way. Teachers are often protective of their classrooms as people are of their own homes because classroom visits from others are out of the ordinary. Because peer visits are more rare than administration visits, teachers could potentially link the objective of peer visits to those of administrator visits. Teachers might feel that anyone visiting might do so in an evaluative way to take information back to administration or other staff rather than to simply learn by observing. In other words, the climate of isolation can work against a free exchange of ideas.

Schools need to define what teachers are learning in direct connection with student learning and to link peer observation to necessary learning rather than unnecessary inconvenience. The school must focus on stated goals. Without clear goals created with teacher input, measurable outcomes, and a fixed timeline, teachers will continue as they have in the past, not understanding why others would be in their "territory" for professional development purposes.

ONGOING SUPPORT AND DIALOGUE

Ongoing support and dialogue can be fostered in a climate of shared commitment to student progress. The support needs to be offered regularly and the benefits of such support should be a part of regular conversation at the site. Ongoing support was perceived as beneficial at the three schools via out-of-classroom support staff and dialogue opportunities. Requests for help were honored and teachers appreciated the extra suggestions that were possible since support staff were not encumbered with classes of their own. A clear picture of what support is available should be a regular aspect of staff meetings as well as opportunities to dialogue.

Agendas generally drive discussions at staff meetings and are too top-down, leaving little room for dialogue. Others viewed meetings as crucial times when tensions could be alleviated by raising "burning" issues. The last item on the agenda was typically "other," where any staff member could raise a question or issue. Teachers in the study revealed that those who raised "other" issues were viewed as lengthening the meeting unnecessarily. Although these "other" issues were brought up for good reasons, every staff member did not typically value them. For this reason, the use of dialogue as an ongoing support tool needs to be incorporated into the culture of the school and not viewed as an unnecessary extra.

FEEDBACK

Experienced teachers in the study did not receive many classroom visits by administrative or support staff simply because they were viewed as competent. More attention was given to teachers who were less skilled. As a result, those who appeared to do well did not get as significant an amount of feedback. Experienced teachers recognize their need to learn, and desire specific feedback to enhance their practice, rather than mere platitudes.

Experienced teachers in the study did not receive many classroom visits by administrative or support staff simply because they were viewed as competent. More attention was given to teachers who were less skilled.

There are a variety of ways the need for feedback can be addressed. Since experience is respected over position when feedback is given, the peer observation opportunities that may lead to dialogue can help fill this need. The use of out-of-the-classroom staff to provide feedback as well as regular visits by administrators to all teachers can enhance practice as well. Regularly scheduled times for teacher dialogue within the workday can provide feedback to teachers in addition to opportunities for practice-driven reflection.

REFLECTIVE DIALOGUE

Reflective dialogue was incorporated into meetings to a limited extent, typically when work samples were reviewed by groups of teachers. Teachers felt opportunities for reflection were rare and staff meetings were typically too agenda driven to present information to teachers rather than to allow reflective dialogue on the effectiveness of their teaching.

There is a great need for reflection and dialogue opportunities to be incorporated into the workday. Finding ways to meet increasingly diverse student needs requires regular thought and planning, much like exercise and practice prior to competing in an athletic event are required for those who seek to do well. A school climate conducive to reflection and dialogue enhances drive toward improvement in the area of focus. The tone of seriousness about teaching and improvement underscores the feeling that every staff member is responsible for the collective achievement of the student body.

CONSIDERATIONS ADDRESSED BY SUCCESSFUL PROFESSIONAL DEVELOPMENT PROGRAMS

1. Is there an example of a time when your site administrators showed above-average commitment to a new program at your site? How would such commitment be shown in connection with ongoing professional development?
2. Under what conditions has your staff shown a collective energy in connection to professional development?
3. How would teachers respond to consistent dialogue opportunities? Would it be viewed as reducing individuality?

Chapter Nine

Practical Recommendations to Improve Teacher Learning

Many steps must be taken to shift the school culture from one of traditional isolation to a climate of ongoing professional development. To assist this process, fourteen recommendations follow.

RECOMMENDATIONS

1. The Climate of Ongoing Learning Must Be Aligned with a Shared Schoolwide Focus

A shared focus is a schoolwide commitment directly connected to student learning. The idea of a student learning connection related to a variety of professional development activities provides a stark contrast to the structure of traditional professional development efforts. Traditional professional development was largely unproductive because the ideas presented were not necessarily going to be viewed as vibrant parts of the school culture. Rather, the ideas were often viewed as optional since, in the traditional culture of isolation, no one would be around to provide feedback on implementation.

> **The vision and focus of the school has to be taken seriously. Allow the airing of questions—even if some emphasize failure of the innovation—and then brainstorm and publicly implement solutions.**

Once collaboratively established, the vision and focus of the school has to be taken seriously. Allow the airing of questions—even if some emphasize failure of the innovation—and then brainstorm and publicly implement solutions. By not incorporating solutions applicable to all students, the schoolwide focus may be perceived as only effective with specific groups of students. A healthy dialogue-based environment excludes the input of no one. Since all teachers have input and are readily expressing their needs and opinions, a higher level of shared responsibility emerges, which intensifies the clear importance of ongoing professional development. The group collectively wants to help each other improve in connection with the schoolwide focus.

Ongoing learning involves recognition of teacher learning needs. Teachers need to be aware that it is safe and beneficial for them to expose their own learning needs. Experienced teachers often use a variety of ways to evaluate student work. Teachers realize the work that students produce can often be no better than the quality of instruction they provide. As a result, student work indicates teacher learning needs in relation to the schoolwide focus. In this environment, it is beneficial to calibrate the work with curricular standards to ensure assignments are appropriate to the grade level taught.

> **Teachers need to be aware that it is safe and beneficial for them to expose their own learning needs.**

The connection of teacher learning needs to schoolwide goals requires firm establishment because it will act as a barometer, indicating areas where more dialogue and training are needed. This constant reevaluation of teacher learning needs would typically not lead the site astray from its schoolwide focus, but rather strengthen the necessity of improvement along the journey toward predetermined goals. The drive to reassess teacher learning needs reveals whether the commitment to a culture of professional learning is permeating the roots or merely the topsoil.

> **Ongoing dialogue leads teachers to capitalize on the expertise of others within the school.**

Ongoing learning must remain at the forefront as teachers analyze student work, linking student performance to teacher performance. Problem solving and dialogue about learning issues are commonplace either in teams or as a whole faculty. The sense of responsibility for the success of every student motivates regular dialogue. Ongoing dialogue leads teachers to capitalize on the expertise of others within the school.

Dialogue regarding improvement leads teachers to avidly seek out research and best practices that will help themselves and others, especially when given the time to do so during the school day. These best practices form the basis for the professional development activities monitored in relation to schoolwide goals and student progress. This type of embedded professional development works against the fate of many innovations that fail due to perceived overall unimportance by staff and administration. Clearly, innovations that fizzle out were not incorporated into the school climate in a meaningful way.

School-based educators will be more motivated to learn if they themselves identify the problem, dilemma, or need on the basis of their understanding of how well students are learning.

Professional development needs to have meaning specific to the school site itself. Buy-in is key to gaining commitment to a shared purpose and focus. "School-based educators will be more motivated to learn if they themselves identify the problem, dilemma, or need on the basis of their understanding of how well students are learning" (Hawley and Valli 2000, 7).

Traditional professional development has rarely been linked to schoolwide focus. Most workshops were organized by someone outside of the school setting and centered on low-level teaching skills. Follow-up was rare because the presentations themselves were infrequently connected to the learning problems encountered by the school sites as well as due to the lack of time assigned for dialogue, observation, and feedback. Each school site is unique and serves students with distinct difficulties. No one knows the difficulties of the students better than the classroom teachers. For this reason, the teachers need to be involved in determining the schoolwide focus as well as the way teachers are trained. The ensuing training in specific strategies helps bridge the gap between current achievement levels and the school's goals.

2. Create a Site-Based Professional Development Plan

A professional development plan must show how the various professional development strategies will help students meet instructional goals at set times throughout the year. Elements of the plan should include the types of ongoing support teachers will receive as well as the ways data will be collected and analyzed. Ongoing support must include peer observations, regular times for reflection and dialogue, and consistent feedback on the incorporation of teaching strategies.

> **Elements of the plan should include the types of ongoing support teachers will receive as well as the ways data will be collected and analyzed.**

The plan should list the various staff members who are responsible for assorted details, since one person cannot be responsible for every detail in the plan. Key players include those who will coordinate work sample reviews for their grade level, those who will provide input on meeting agendas, those who will help design teacher activities as needs arise from reviews of student work, and other details.

3. Create Benchmarks

Benchmark dates need to be assigned to give teachers and students a target toward which to aim. The dates for particular accomplishments within the schoolwide focus will guide teachers' efforts as well as the training opportunities throughout the year. For example, if teachers want students to be able to display particular writing skills by winter break, times for analysis of student work samples must be determined, and outside speakers or staff members might conduct training sessions on how to incorporate various writing strategies for particular groups of students—all of which lead up to the date when results are expected. Benchmarks provide a sense of direction often missing from professional development activities. Clear, realistic student outcomes set up as learning targets motivate instructional efforts and close assessment of student work.

Benchmark dates need to be assigned to give teachers and students a target toward which to aim. Benchmarks provide a sense of direction often missing from professional development activities.

These benchmark dates need to be bolstered by determining when progress will be reviewed publicly. Teachers and other instructional staff need to know if their efforts are on target or not. At such points, teachers might choose to adjust their plans for the remainder of the year and adjust future benchmarks. More review might be needed or too much time might have been taken for certain outcomes. The plan must be seen as flexible and based on teachers' needs. If the plan is out of alignment in some way, it can be changed based on staff input.

In addition to benchmark goals, a review of the year's progress needs to be in place. Multiple measures should be used. A quantitative view can be taken by simply tallying the number of times a teacher has observed another teacher, the number of times teachers have reviewed work samples, the number of times set aside for reflection and dialogue during staff meetings or outside staff meetings, and other measurable professional development activities. Work samples, standardized tests, and other criteria assist in assessment of student outcomes. Publicly reviewed results should accurately reflect reality, whether positive or less than positive. Problems not discussed openly will only give way to larger problems later. These issues need resolution through instructional adaptation readily available within the culture of ongoing professional development.

The culture needs to reflect that professional development is happening all the time. Teachers need to compare notes during common planning periods. Professional development days need to be spread out over time rather than bunched at the beginning or end of the school year. Regular release time must be provided to allow teachers to observe one another. Computer network systems should have access to teacher learning resources specifically linked to the schoolwide focus and link teachers to one another to exchange lesson plans, brainstorm ideas, and so forth. The overall expectation of all staff is that learning is ongoing.

The culture needs to reflect that professional development is happening all the time.

4. Ensure That Professional Development Efforts Involving Peer Observations, Reflective Dialogue, and Feedback Are Nonjudgmental in Nature and Will Promote an Exchange of Ideas

Peer observations, reflective dialogue, and feedback opportunities should not be opportunities for teachers to evaluate one another. This study advocates a model similar to brainstorming or therapy where the context is nonjudgmental. These activities have far less of a chance for success if they are undertaken in an atmosphere where the teacher is "on the spot" by becoming the subject of discussion. Ideas and teaching strategies should be topics of discussion rather than the performance of a particular teacher. It is recommended that the nonevaluative nature of these activities be clarified from the start.

> **Ideas and teaching strategies should be topics of discussion rather than the performance of a particular teacher.**

5. Clarify the Perception That Peer Observations Are Part of the Learning Culture

Teachers readily admitted that observing others could be considered a nuisance and an intrusion. If learning is highly valued, then the activities that support teacher learning are not a nuisance to the staff but an adaptation from a previous culture of isolation. New strategies cannot become part of school culture unless training is ongoing and realistic demonstrations provide concrete examples while also stimulating further discussion. Peer observations provide a unique avenue for seeing demonstrations that clarify the innovation and the basis for further professional discussion. Peer observations are credited with increasing retention within the teaching profession (Odell and Ferraro 1992). It is a bold move away from isolationism.

> **Peer observations are credited with increasing retention within the teaching profession.**

Isolation is the enemy of instructional improvement. In a culture of ongoing learning, teachers are no longer "self-contained" and territorial but ready to observe and be observed. Such vulnerability leads to issues of trust since a lack of such isolation might be considered a radical, uncomfortable innovation. Trust is established in any relationship through communication. To gain trust among staff, the communication must be purposeful and lead to an understanding of the rationale, purposes, and processes about the ongoing learning culture (Fullan 1999).

The role of peer observations in the school culture needs emphasis through administrative actions and not solely discussion. Ensuring release time via out-of-classroom teachers, substitutes, or other methods of relieving teachers themselves to observe are ways administrators may show the importance of this learning strategy. All school leaders should clearly articulate the benefits and the effort put into the innovation to help all staff recognize it as part of the culture.

> **The professional development literature states that peer observation "is typically more potent than formal teacher education."**

The professional development literature states that peer observation "is typically more potent than formal teacher education" (Ball and Cohen 1999, 5). Another finding correlated with the literature is that "teachers who were observed and who observed others frequently rated such activity as having a strong impact on their own development—but very few teachers actually did it" (Little 1999, 248).

> **But very few teachers actually did it.**

6. Create a System for Classroom Coverage to Emphasize the Importance of Peer Observations in the Ongoing Learning Culture and to Create an Infrastructure That Will Outlast the Leader

If the goals are meaningful to administration, classroom coverage is automatically arranged through a preset system rather than viewed as a sudden inconvenience when the issue arises. The preset system would involve how a teacher is to schedule a visit to another classroom and who will cover the observing teacher's class. A comprehensive system invites new and experienced teachers to take advantage of it. Infrastructure installed to ensure the ability of teachers to take advantage of the strategy speaks volumes regarding the value of this type of teacher learning.

> **If the goals are meaningful to administration, classroom coverage is automatically arranged through a preset system rather than viewed as a sudden inconvenience when the issue arises.**

Infrastructure needs to be established within the ongoing professional development system. As part of the school culture, ongoing dialogue opportunities, peer observations, and other strategies should not rest on the efforts of one individual instructional leader. Although an instructional leader can start great things, danger lies in a lack of infrastructure that could lead to potential disintegration of the program once that leader is no longer at the site. Which staff members will care for particular organizational needs, such as determining how and when data will be collected and received? What documentation will be expected of the reviews such that progress can be tracked? How will results be publicly displayed and discussed? If the site believes ongoing professional development has lasting benefits for staff and students, this plan must reflect long-term learning concerns regardless of changes in school leadership.

7. Ensure Productive Time during Reflective Dialogue Opportunities

A critical component for any ongoing learning environment is the creation of regular opportunities to reflect and dialogue about professional issues. These opportunities are currently missing in many schools. Even in the three schools in this study where some reflective dialogue was already occurring, teachers felt it was not enough. The three schools were involved in ongoing training but the school leaders did not ensure the existence of dialogue opportunities beyond occasional grade-level meetings. Teachers in the study recognized the value of learning from one another. Reflective dialogue enlivened the practice of many teachers in the study and enabled them to mine the expertise of one another. Such mining might take place more regularly if the opportunities to do so were available.

> **Reflective dialogue enlivened the practice of many teachers in the study and enabled them to mine the expertise of one another.**

Administrators must ensure productive use of time during reflective dialogue opportunities. Simple strategies can make meetings more productive. Staff should have input on agendas and a proactive role in discussion rather than merely listening to announcements. Specific content areas provide the focus of currently scheduled meetings and professional development time rather than administration and information dissemination.

Reflection and dialogue at faculty meetings could be possible through a variety of ways. Administrative matters limited to bulletin boards, daily postings, e-mail, or other announcement/nondiscussion-related methods might free up time for meetings on the schoolwide focus. Agenda setting as a shared effort between administration and teachers can enhance productivity of meetings specifically designated for talking, thinking, sharing, and reflecting on instructional issues. Single-issue faculty meetings moderated by peer-selected faculty members could readily direct attention to instructional strategies related to the schoolwide focus. Or time might be allotted for reflection and dialogue during the school day.

> **Single-issue faculty meetings moderated by peer-selected faculty members could readily direct attention to instructional strategies related to the schoolwide focus.**

One school in the study at times incorporates reflection and dialogue into the school day by outlining the discussion topics ahead of time. Time at this school is "banked," in that students attend school a larger number of minutes over a four-day period, such that the fifth day requires a smaller number of minutes. This allows more time for teacher professional development during the paid workday of teachers. Teachers perceive banked times used for dialogue as effective, useful opportunities that are so out of the ordinary that they feel "like a bonus," according to many.

The following are ways to create more professional development time within the school day:

Use substitutes or additional available staff to release teachers for professional development purposes

Start the student day later once a week, with the longer four days ensuring legislated numbers of instructional minutes are met

Set up common conference and planning times

Arrange appropriate supervision during assemblies and guest speakers so
teachers can collaborate

8. Increase Time for Professional Development

The creation and maintenance of an ongoing learning culture requires increasing professional development time in a variety of ways. Restricting time required for nonprofessional duties could free up more time for professional development. This could include keeping fundraising activities out of the teachers' hands and having support staff available to ensure office machines, supplies, and other necessities are in working order or readily available rather than relying on teachers to find and maintain their own resources. A "substitute bank" of thirty to forty days per year established in collaboration with the district, from which teachers can withdraw, might support special professional development activities and other development projects. Grants written to foundations or other funding agencies might secure monies to fund release time for planning and dialogue purposes.

> **Restricting time required for nonprofessional duties could free up more time for professional development.**

Attacking the problem of insufficient time during the school day is critical. Those within the teaching profession are not adequately compensated for time outside of the contracted workday. Aside from the typical planning and grading needs, teachers also deserve time to collaborate. Collaboration-inspired dialogue provides ongoing support, which makes the job of teaching easier and more pleasurable. Many in the study felt that teachers generally had to give up aspects of their own personal lives to have time for dialogue and collaboration. A culture of ongoing professional development requires activities during the school day, rather than in addition to classroom hours. Collaboration usually saves time by helping solve problems expediently and by sharing resources.

Schools that incorporate dialogue time into the school day make teachers feel, as one teacher in the study put it, like they are "getting a bonus."

Dialogue time along with the help of out-of-the-classroom support staff gives teachers a clear idea that the program, innovation, or focus honors their learning needs and the success of the entire school.

Various strategies can free instructional time during the school day for professional development purposes. Teaming teachers formally and informally to instruct for one another could free time for dialogue. Classes could combine with a coordinated community event, such as guest speakers doing activities or performances, so teachers could collaborate. Parents, business members, or community volunteers could provide alternative activities or enrichment programs.

They should not feel guilty when away from students for professional development purposes.

Teachers must adjust to the fact that they are always educators, even when not in front of their classes. They should not feel guilty when away from students for professional development purposes. Professional learning is easily sustained if provided in addition to all current teacher duties. Professional development, when realistic and realistically paced, does not burden teachers but provides a stimulating relief as new ideas encourage and energize them. (See appendix B for notes regarding professional development within year-round school calendars.)

9. Involve All Teachers in Reflective Dialogue

When involving the entire faculty, the transfer rate of an innovation into classroom practice approaches 100 percent, whereas it is lower when only part of the faculty has the opportunity to participate in professional development activities.

When the schoolwide focus is determined collaboratively, all teachers are involved in discussion of the innovation rather than only those teachers who choose to participate. When involving the entire faculty, the transfer rate of an innovation into classroom practice approaches 100 percent, whereas it is lower when only part of the faculty has the opportunity to participate in professional development activities (Joyce and Showers 1995).

Involvement of all teachers in dialogue has value even in the face of potential argument and debate. Conjecture, weighing of rationales, critiquing, and explorations of viewpoints are all part of inquiry. Active dialogue should incorporate a variety of viewpoints in productive disagreements, which increases understanding and diffuses tensions that build over time.

> **Conjecture, weighing of rationales, critiquing, and explorations of viewpoints are all part of inquiry.**

10. Reflective Dialogue Needs to Be Directly Linked to the Schoolwide Focus

> **Teachers are more eager to participate in professional development activities if they feel students would benefit and that they themselves would grow professionally.**

In the past, teachers have spent hours receiving training in an isolated topic not directly related to student learning difficulties and had no need to dialogue about the sessions afterwards. Because ongoing learning opportunities for reflection and dialogue are directly related to a clear schoolwide focus, however, teachers must understand how mastery of the schoolwide focus can result from reflective dialogue. Teachers are thinking about learning issues and comparing notes on strategies directly affecting their students. This type of reflective dialogue could include speaking openly about specific content areas, problems students might confront in learning that content, and instructional strategies that address anticipated problems or solutions. Such exchanges enhance interest in ongoing learning. Teachers are more eager to participate in professional development activities if they feel students would benefit and that they themselves would grow professionally.

11. Provide Regular, Specific Feedback for Both Experienced and New Teachers

> **Feedback can be verbal, in writing, or by e-mail.**

Both experienced and new teachers in the study desired regular feedback on their teaching practices. Feedback can be verbal, in writing, or by e-mail. Feedback ideally clarifies ideas, expectations, and possibilities. Teachers should expect and readily accept feedback as part of the ongoing learning environment. The source of the feedback is less critical than its substance since the free flow of ideas is part of an optimal work environment.

Detailing next steps provides an avenue for dialogue between out-of-classroom teachers or administrators who provide feedback and the classroom practitioners.

Platitudes must be avoided even though suggestions are sometimes difficult to think of for experienced teachers who consistently engage all students. Actual suggestions or comments regarding lesson details might spur a teacher to explore different teaching methods. When many areas need improvement, incremental feedback could be most useful. Detailing next steps provides an avenue for dialogue between out-of-classroom teachers or administrators who provide feedback and the classroom practitioners. The following-up of next steps during future observations over time works well for teachers with a long list of weak areas. Dialogue is so crucial that anyone providing feedback must be available later to listen to ideas of the observed teacher. The intent is not to evaluate but to improve overall practice. In fact, teachers find nonevaluative peer feedback situations very useful compared to infrequent evaluative feedback situations and desire more feedback to consistently improve practice. When all available support staff members disseminate feedback, the chance of giving suggestions to more teachers is greater than if feedback is provided solely by administrators.

The intent is not to evaluate but to improve overall practice.

12. Keep in Mind That Knowledgeable Feedback Is Respected over Positional Feedback

Specifics regarding instructional strategies from experienced practitioners have lasting impact over a simple positive or negative evaluation from an administrator.

The data frequently showed that teachers desire feedback from knowledgeable sources. Specifics regarding instructional strategies from experienced practitioners have lasting impact over a simple positive or negative evaluation from an administrator. Teachers desire pointed feedback from someone who is credible.

Teachers desire pointed feedback from someone who is credible.

The majority of experienced teachers in this study desired more feedback than what was given. They would have liked to hear input on potential areas of deficiency and receive incremental "next step" suggestions.

13. Authentic Situations Need to Be Used over Artificial Appointments

Experienced teachers in the study felt that drop-in times create more authentic observations than preset appointments.

Experienced teachers in the study felt that drop-in times create more authentic observations than preset appointments. Appointments are the traditional forums for staged observations. These typically do not give an accurate picture of what everyday teaching and learning look like in that classroom. Content presented, student interaction, and assignments given form the basis for everyday teaching and learning. Everyday teaching might not be as carefully prepared or elaborate but that is when the feedback is most applicable. The "I'll be looking for . . ." warnings before making observations create the sense that teachers need to prepare differently because ordinary teaching and learning won't be enough. To ensure realistic improvement of everyday teaching and learning, preset appointments should not provide the basis for critiques. The ongoing, everyday practice of authentic teaching and learning is the basis for genuine criticism. Yet the criticism of peers could pose difficulties.

Everyday teaching might not be as carefully prepared or elaborate but that is when the feedback is most applicable.

Peer observations present potential teacher union conflicts. Teacher unions need foreknowledge of the intent of peer observations because uninformed teachers will likely sense these observations could impact their evaluations. The peer observations must always remain nonevaluative in nature. The observing teacher visits to learn from what he or she sees rather than to provide direct feedback to the teacher being observed.

> **Peer observations present potential teacher union conflicts and must always remain nonevaluative in nature.**

14. Celebrate Results but Plan Ahead

Recognition must be in place if the effort is legitimate. When administrators do not recognize the work being done by failing to attend dialogue sessions, review work samples, publicly review progress, and celebrate the efforts, teachers lose their drive to continue. The professional development efforts need to be consistently in the conversation of staff, students, and parents in order to be significant.

> **Recognition must be in place if the effort is legitimate.**

According to the data, a lack of discussion about the innovation will make the environment seem no different from previous years and old reform efforts that have drifted away. In essence, the value and importance of the effort will be lost if results are not visible. Even if small, improvement requires visible recognition. The concrete results seen from the first benchmark goal will drive the remainder of the effort. Until the school can see the impact on student learning, the shift to a collaborative ongoing learning culture will not have staying power (Fullan 1999).

> **The concrete results seen from the first benchmark goal will drive the remainder of the effort.**

Benchmarks may be reached with more ease or difficulty than anticipated, or not reached at all. Flexibility to restructure the type of training sessions or needed professional development speakers is critical. Flexibility in this case means the ability to plan ahead as well as the willingness to change the plan if the need arises. Realignment of the plan at each benchmark in anticipation of activities for the following year should be in the discussion at various times throughout the year. Creating an ongoing learning environment means having the conversation at staff meetings signify that this environment is not going away. While the plan, area of focus, and specific activities might change according to teacher needs, the continuous professional learning will not.

CONSIDERATIONS ADDRESSED BY SUCCESSFUL PROFESSIONAL DEVELOPMENT PROGRAMS

1. How would authentic assessments of teacher learning needs be carried out effectively at your site? Would it take the form of a survey, leadership team discussion, focus group, or some other means?
2. Which grade-level teams seem more driven to accomplish collaborative goals? How could their energy be transferred to others?
3. How could potential staff apathy toward dialogue and other professional development activities be combated?
4. How would your site best determine an area of focus and create a professional development plan?
5. Who would be willing to devote creative energy to the creation of this plan?

Epilogue

Learning impacts action. Teachers act based on what they know has worked in the past and what they are reasonably confident will work in the future. Without new ideas, the desire on the part of teachers to try new things is limited. By immersing teachers in a culture of ongoing learning, the likelihood of implementing new ideas increases.

The dramatic shift from a culture of isolation to ongoing professional development requires agreement on the schoolwide focus and the direction taken to enhance student achievement in that area. The professionally invigorating climate, schoolwide focus, and benchmark goals necessary to impact student learning should be as expected at every school as the morning flag salute. While such a culture is relatively uncommon in schools today and despite increasing daily challenges, this shift must begin to give teachers an environment where they learn best.

POTENTIAL CHALLENGES

1. Overload. Some teachers may have difficulty with so much change at the school site. Most are accustomed to comfortable isolation without intense involvement with others. Teachers need to collaborate and, by doing so, provide support for themselves and their students. Administrators need to be sensitive to this enormous shift through support and flexibility.
2. Lack of initial buy-in. Because creating a new culture of ongoing professional development takes time, there is a great need to not promise

too much from changes. Results will often be meager at first. Those who hear that staggering improvement will take place soon may be the first to give up when results are not immediate. Deep-rooted change takes time and will be long lasting if teachers understand that the evidence will likely not be noticeable in the short term.

3. What should be done when teachers feel overwhelmed and, for instance, don't want to review the work samples? The follow-up efforts by administration and others on staff to encourage the work will have an effect. If administration and other key staff members do not show intense interest, then teachers will perceive this innovation as unimportant.

FUTURE ISSUES TO EXPLORE

1. How schools in other countries afford time for dialogue and planning. Studies of Asian and European schools show teachers are in charge of classes 50 to 60 percent of the time, leaving a large amount of time for professional development activities compared to American schools (DSEA 1994).

2. Funding changes that need to occur to make these recommendations regular realities of every school site. Many schools are not able to afford an out-of-the-classroom teacher to provide support to experienced and new teachers. Release time provided by substitutes can become costly unless a financial structure is in place to carry the costs related to this type of professional development activity.

3. The changes that districts and unions must undertake to facilitate dialogue and collaboration time during the school day, more professional development days without sacrificing instructional days, and accompanying policy issues. Large and minute policy changes are undertaken through collaborative efforts in most districts between administration and teacher unions. For agreement to be reached, a foundation of understanding of the importance of professional development to all stakeholders must be clarified.

Appendix A

CONTRASTING THE OLD WITH THE NEW

Quality	Traditional	Ongoing Model
Peer observations	Rare, for those really needing help; an imposition on others; uncomfortable	New and experienced teachers alike visit one another to gain ideas
Ongoing support	Approach administrators or peers when you need help; partnered with mentor-type teacher	Out-of-classroom teacher available to provide assistance
Consistent feedback	Administrative responsibility; rare to have a visit from anyone else	With peer observations and out-of-classroom support staff, more opportunity for meaningful, nonadministrative feedback
Reflective dialogue	Not typically a part of staff meetings	Opportunities to dialogue and reflect on practice are scheduled and viewed as important

Appendix B

NOTES REGARDING YEAR-ROUND CALENDARS

The teachers in the study were concerned about the reduced number of instructional days they had due to the current year-round calendar. Many districts undertake the valid option of extending the school year to accommodate more professional development days without sacrificing instructional days.

Schools on the year-round calendar can use the track system to their advantage. Teachers should be encouraged to call one another and observe one another during off-track time. Some teachers in the study took advantage of this idea even though they were not paid for their time. Others did not know this was a possibility and felt it was not publicized very much. In a climate of ongoing learning, every opportunity must be used.

In addition to peer observations, teachers can also meet together on days when one track is preparing to return and another is leaving. The communication between groups can give great insight into the area of focus. This insight is available because those who are going off track appear to be ahead in the curriculum than those returning. Teachers exchanged ideas about what curricular areas required more time, how to address the needs of English learners, and other instructional issues.

References

Ackerman, R., G. Donaldson, and R. Bogert. 1996. *Making sense as a school leader*. San Francisco: Jossey-Bass.

Ball, D. L., and D. K. Cohen. 1999. Developing practice, developing practitioners: Toward a practice-based theory of professional education. In *Teaching as the learning profession: Handbook of policy and practice*, edited by L. Darling-Hammond, 3–32. San Francisco: Jossey-Bass.

Brooks, M., and J. Brooks. 1993. *In search of understanding: The case for constructivist classrooms*. Alexandria, Va.: Association for Supervision and Curriculum Development.

Danielson, C., and T. L. McGreal. 2000. *Teacher evaluation: To enhance professional practice*. Alexandria, Va.: Association for Supervision and Curriculum Development.

Darling-Hammond, L., and M. W. McLaughlin. 1999. Investing in teaching as a learning profession: Policy problems and prospects. In *Teaching as the learning profession: Handbook of policy and practice*, edited by L. Darling-Hammond, 376–411. San Francisco: Jossey-Bass.

DSEA. 1994. *It is about time!* at www.ilt.columbia.edu/k12/tpi/timekit/iat.html (accessed Spring 2001).

Fullan, M. 1982. *The meaning of educational change*. New York: Teachers College Press.

———. 1999. *Change forces: The sequel.* London: Falmer Press.

Fullan, M., and S. Stiegelbauer. 1991. *The new meaning of educational change.* New York: Teachers College Press.

Hawley, W., and L. Valli. 1999. The essentials of effective professional development: A new consensus. In *Teaching as the learning profession: Handbook of policy and practice*, edited by L. Darling-Hammond, 127–50. San Francisco: Jossey-Bass.

———. 2000. Learner-centered professional development. *Phi Delta Kappa Research Bulletin* no. 27 (August): 7–10.

Holly, P. 1991. Action research: The missing link in the creation of schools as centers of inquiry. In *Staff development for education in the '90s.* 2nd ed. Edited by A. Lieberman and L. Miller, 133–57. New York: Teachers College Press.

Joyce, B. and B Showers. 1995. *Student achievement through staff development.* 2nd ed. White Plains, N.Y.: Longman.

Lieberman, A., and L. Miller. 1991. Revisiting the social realities of teaching. In *Staff development for education in the '90s.* 2nd ed. Edited by A. Lieberman and L. Miller, 92–112. New York: Teachers College Press.

Little, J. W. 1999. Organizing schools for teacher learning. In *Teaching as the learning profession: Handbook of policy and practice,* edited by L. Darling-Hammond, 233–62. San Francisco: Jossey-Bass.

McLaughlin, M. W. 1991. Enabling staff development: What have we learned? In *Staff development for education in the '90s.* 2nd ed. Edited by A. Lieberman and L. Miller, 61–82. New York: Teachers College Press.

Meier, D. 1992. Reinventing teaching. *Teachers College Record* 93, no. 4: 594–609.

Munson, B. 1998. Peers observing peers: The better way to observe teachers. *Contemporary Education* 69, no. 2: 108–11.

Odell, S., and D. Ferraro. 1992. Teacher mentoring and teacher retention. *Journal of Teacher Education* 43, no. 3: 200–204.

Renyi, J. 1998. Building learning into the teaching job. *Educational Leadership* 55, no. 5: 70–74.

Senge, P. 1999. *The dance of change.* New York: Doubleday.

Sparks, H. 1997. *A new vision for staff development.* Alexandria, Va.: Association for Supervision and Curriculum Development.

Suggested Readings

Baker, R., and B. Showers. 1984. The effects of a coaching strategy on teachers' transfer of training to classroom practice: A six-month follow up study. Paper presented at the American Educational Research Association, New Orleans, La.

Cooper, M. 1991. Stretching the limits of our vision: Staff development and the transformation of schools. In *Staff development for education in the '90s*, 2nd ed., edited by A. Lieberman and L. Miller, 83–91. New York: Teachers College Press.

Darling-Hammond, L. 1995. Policies that support professional development in an era of reform. *Phi Delta Kappan* 76, no. 8: 597.

Eisenback, R., and R. Curry. 1999. The emotional reaction to classroom visitation and peer coaching. *Journal of Management Education* 23, no. 4: 416–28.

Elmore, R., and D. Burney. 1999. Investing in teacher learning: Staff development and instructional improvement. In *Teaching as the learning profession: Handbook of policy and practice*, edited by L. Darling-Hammond, 263–91. San Francisco: Jossey-Bass.

Greenfield, T. A. 1995. Improving chances for successful educational reform. *Education* 115, no. 3: 464.

Guskey, T. R. 1985. Staff development and teacher change. *Educational Leadership* (April): 57–60.

Joyce, B., and Showers, B. 1980. Improving in-service training: The messages of research. *Educational Leadership* 37 (February): 379–85.

Kinsella, K. 1995. Peer coaching teaching: Colleagues supporting professional growth across the disciplines. *To Improve the Academy* 14: 107–24.

Lawrence, G. 1974. *Patterns of effective in-service education: A state of the art summary of research on materials and procedures for changing teacher behaviors in in-service education*. Tallahassee: Florida State Department of Education. ED 176 424.

Little, J. W. 1982. Norms of collegiality and experimentation: Workplace conditions of school success. *American Educational Research Journal* 19, no. 3: 325–40.

———. 1986. Seductive images and organizational realities in professional development. In *Rethinking school improvement*, edited by A. Lieberman, 26–44. New York: Teachers College Press.

———. 1993. Teachers' professional development in a climate of educational reform. *Educational Evaluation and Policy Analysis* 15, no. 2: 129–51.

Lohman, M. C., and N. H. Woolf. 1998. Toward a culture of teacher learning in the public schools: A human resource development perspective. *Teaching and Change* 5, no. 3–4: 276–93.

NPEAT. 2000. *Revisioning professional development*. Oxford, Ohio: National Staff Development Council.

Oja, S. N. 1991. Adult development: Insights on staff development. In *Staff development for education in the '90s*. 2nd ed. Edited by A. Lieberman and L. Miller, 37–60. New York: Teachers College Press.

Purkey, S. C., and M. S. Smith. 1983. Effective schools: A review. *The Elementary School Journal* 83, no. 4: 427–52.

Richert, A. E. 1991. Using teacher cases for reflection and enhanced understanding. In *Staff development for education in the '90s*. 2nd ed. Edited by A. Lieberman and L. Miller, 113–32. New York: Teachers College Press.

Schmoker, M. 2003. First things first: Demystifying data analysis. *Educational Leadership* 60, no. 5: 22–24.

Schon, D. A. 1987. *Educating the reflective practitioner*. San Francisco: Jossey-Bass.

Schwartz, J. 1991. Developing an ethos for professional growth: Politics and programs. In *Staff development for education in the '90s*. 2nd ed. Edited by A. Lieberman and L. Miller, 184–92. New York: Teachers College Press.

Showers, B., and Joyce, B. 1980. Improving in-service training: The messages of research. *Educational Leadership* 37 (February): 379–85.

———. 1996. The evolution of peer coaching. *Educational Leadership* 54, no. 3: 12–16.

Stevens, R. J., N. A. Madden, R. E. Slavin, and A. M. Farnish. 1987. Cooperative integrated reading and composition: Two field experiments. *Reading Research Quarterly* 22: 433–54.

Stevenson, R. B. 1987. Staff development for effective secondary schools: A synthesis of research. *Teaching and Teacher Education* 3, no. 3: 233–48.

Stiggins, R. J. 2002. Assessment crisis: The absence of assessment for learning. *Phi Delta Kappan* 83, no. 10: 758–65.

Sykes, G. 1999. Teacher and student learning: Strengthening their connection. In *Teaching as the learning profession: Handbook of policy and practice*, edited by L. Darling-Hammond, 151–79. San Francisco: Jossey-Bass.

Wasley, P. A. 1991. The practical work of teacher leaders: Assumptions, attitudes, and acrophobia. In *Staff development for education in the '90s*. 2nd ed. Edited by A. Lieberman and L. Miller, 158–83. New York: Teachers College Press.

Index

About the Author

Edward P. Fiszer was born and raised in Los Angeles, California, and has always shown an interest in education. Aside from part-time jobs while attending high school and college, he has never worked outside of an educational setting. Edward received his bachelor of arts degree in history at UCLA and a multiple-subject teaching credential at California State University, Northridge. While serving as an elementary school teacher and English language development specialist in Burbank, he attended the Educational Leadership Academy at Pepperdine University for a master of science degree in education administration. He returned to UCLA for a doctorate through the Educational Leadership Program while working as a site administrator in Palmdale. Upon completion of his doctorate, Edward became principal of a school in Santa Clarita and teaches graduate-level courses in education. Other than exercise (he has completed numerous marathons), he enjoys music, film, reading, and writing.